*Promotional
Modeling
101:*

*How to Easily Succeed in
Promotional Modeling*

*By
Kimberly
Fisher*

AUTHOR BIO

Kimberly Fisher is a model, actress and freelance writer based in Beverly Hills, CA. She specializes in luxury travel, lifestyle, beauty and fashion. With extensive travel experience visiting some of the world's most sough-after destinations, Kimberly is truly a connoisseur globetrotter. She has traveled to 39 countries and almost every U.S. state. Her work has appeared in various English print and online media, including Disarray Magazine, NiteGuide Magazine, Ocean View Magazine, 52perfectdays.com, ehow.com tangodiva.com and USAToday.com.

She updates this guide frequently to keep you up to date.

Kimberly Fisher does not accept payments or discounts in exchange for coverage of any sort.

1st Edition, October 2009.
ISBN: 978-0-578-02893-4

The author has done his best to ensure the accuracy and completeness of this guide. However, she can accept no responsibility for any loss, injury, or inconvenience sustained as a result of information or advice in this guide.

Table of Contents

Chapter One:

About Me

Welcome!

Hello Everyone!

I want to first thank you for taking interest in my book. I get hundreds of emails from my website asking the basic questions of getting into promotional modeling and work as a tradeshow spokesperson and promotional model. This will explain some of the basics of getting into the industry and maintaining a prosperous, fulfilling and fun career. I sort of fell into it by accident, and wished I had some kind of guide along the way. To make your life easier, here it is! Best of luck to you in your new career!

Xo,
Kimberly

About Me

I grew up in Anchorage, Alaska. After I did my first promotional "modeling" gig at age fourteen for Coca-Cola, I was hooked, and soon after that I began my adventure as a model.

I have spent the last several years trying out just about everything in the entertainment industry. I have been a beauty queen. I have been very successful as a model, an actress, and a spokesperson for several different companies. I have hosted TV Shows. I've been a music video vixen and a centerfold. I have been a Product Specialist for Lexus and Nitto Tires. I've done voiceovers and radio interviews. I have interviewed celebrities on the red carpet and I have a popular website that has seen over 4 million visitors and at one point was one of the top 100,000 websites *in the world*. I have dabbled in screenwriting, travel writing and producing.

All the while, I have succeeded in being a successful Tradeshow and Promotional Model.

I have spent countless hours over the years researching different agencies and marketing companies, working events, and gathering information for submissions. I hope this guide will help you get a jump-start to your career!

My Tradeshow Resume

01/00	CES	S.V.F. Inc.
02/00	WSA Shoe Show	Diesel Shoes
08/00	WSA Shoe Show	Diesel Shoes
02/01	WSA Shoe Show	Diesel Shoes
03/01	Thompson Financial	Debt Buyers Inc.
08/01	WSA Shoe Show	Diesel Shoes
08/01	MAGIC Show	Diesel Shoes
11/01	AHA	Parexel MMS
01/02	LA Auto Show	Lexus
01/02	Inter. Beauty Show	Farouk
01/02	WSA Shoe Show	Diesel Shoes
02/02	MAGIC Show	Eti'k Fashions
03/02	Cleveland Auto Show	Lexus
04/02	Atlanta Auto Show	Lexus
06/02	IFT	Archer Daniels Mid.
08/02	WSA Shoe Show	Diesel Shoes
11/02	APPEX	Blair Corp.
11/02	Inter. Hair & Spa Show	Farouk
11/02	SFO Auto Show	Lexus
01/03	Houston Auto Show	Lexus
03/03	APEX	Simplamatic
04/03	Minneapolis Auto Show	Lexus
01/04	CES	Sharp Electronics
01/04	AHR Expo	Fedders
02/04	PMA Show	Konica-Minolta
02/04	Wedding Portrait &Photo	Kodak
05/04	E3	Eidios
08/04	WSA Shoe Show	Cynthia Rowley
08/04	ASD/AMD Show	Flip-O
08/04	MAGIC Show	Flip-O
09/04	Inter. Mining Expo	SMC Electrical
10/04	PMA	Kodak
11/04	SEMA	D'Vinci Wheels
02/05	ASD/AMD Show	Flip-O
03/05	Bar & Nightclub Show	Petron
04/05	WestTec	Femco USA
04/05	NAB	MediaLink
04/05	NAB	Intelsat
05/05	E3	Alliance Distribution
10/05	Anaheim Auto Show	Nissan
11/05	SEMA Auto Show	Zenetti Wheels
01/06	LA Auto Show	Nitto Tires
02/06	NHRA Show	Nitto Tires
02/06	Asia's GEM Show	Casino Filipino

03/06	Bar and Nightclub	Sabor Azul
04/06	IAS Mt. Washington	Nitto Tires
04/06	N.A.B.	MediaLinks
05/06	Interop Las Vegas	Aruba Networks
05/06	E3 Show	Atlus Inc.
06/06	Bowl Expo	Quibica AMF
08/06	Shoe Show	NYLA
09/06	American Chemical Soc.	Industrial Biotech
09/06	NOPI Atlanta	Nitto Tires
09/06	HIN SFO	Nitto Tires
10/06	NACS	Fuze Inc.
10/06	ADA	Staino
10/06	SEMA Auto Show	Fuze Inc./NOS
11/06	G2E Show	Digideal Inc.
1/07	AVN Show	VideoRental.com
2/07	Shoe Show	Southpole Inc.
3/07	Nightclub and Bar	Anheiser Busch
3/07	NMRA	Nitto Tires
3/07	ShowWest	Stain-o
4/07	NAB	MediaLinks
5/07	The Cable Show	MTV/BET Networks
5/07	World Ford Challenge	Nitto Tires
5/07	Interop	F5 Networks
6/07	IDDBA	Franklin Foods
6/07	Erotica LA	VideoRental.com
6/07	Bowl Expo	Budweiser
7/07	Ford World Challenge	Nitto Tires
7/07	WSA Shoe Show	Brown Shoe
8/07	NASCAR Expo	Kerner Mobile
10/07	SEMA	BBS Wheels
11/07	NAR	Apple Rock
1/08	CES	Sharp Electronics
2/08	WSA Shoe Show	Brown Shoe
2/08	Bar and Nightclub	Anheiser Busch
2/08	Electronic West	Clockwork Home
3/08	Natural Foods Expo	Sitea Inc.
4/08	CTIA	Powerwave
4/08	NAB	MediaLinks
4/08	Interop	F5 Networks
5/08	The Gourmet Show	Burton Plastics
5/08	ICSC	Pacific Star Capital
5/08	JCK Jewelry Show	U.S. Watch Council
7/08	WSA Shoe Show	Brown Shoe
8/08	Taste of Lexus	Lexus
10/08	Off Road Expo	Toyota
11/08	SEMA	GM

11/08	NV Air Show	GM
1/09	CES	Polytron
1/09	IBS	Protective Products
3/09	Natural Products Expo	Pirates Booty
6/09	CosmoProf	Diamond Towel
7/09	WSA Show Show	Brown Shoe
8/09	Columbus Beauty Show	Diamond Towel
9/09	Birmingham Beauty	Diamond Towel
10/09	NACS Show	Anheiser Busch
1/10	CES Show	Iwave Audio
1/10	ISSE Beauty Show	Diamond Towel
3/10	NYC Beauty Show	Diamond Towel
3/10	Chicago Beauty Show	Diamond Towel
1/11	CES Show	LG Electronics
1/11	NAMM Show	Party Works USA
1/11	ISSE Beauty Show	Diamond Towel

*Tradeshow resume tip: I have seen a couple different layouts for tradeshow resume formats, but this seems like the easiest one for both you and your agents. Date, Show and Company worked for. Some also add the job position. (Hostess, narrarator, etc.)

Chapter 2: About You

About You

What are the benefits of a promotional job?

*Exciting industry
*Flexible schedule
*Meet new people
*Sizable income
*Travel
*Gain new experiences

Qualities you *must* have to succeed in this business:

*Positive Attitude. No one wants to work with a sourpuss all day! Leave the negative energy and problems at home!

*Reliability. No one likes a flake, and they will remember who has been there on time or canceled last minute. Showing responsibility is huge!

Punctuality. Clients have paid for your time, so please respect it. This also applies to being considerate to your other team members on breaks/lunches.

Organization. When you have four different flights, six tradeshows, four promotions, two meetings, and nine auditions and a conference call, it's up to you to keep track.

Networking capabilities. More than half of my work is from my friends. If you are not a good networker, you could hurt your chances of working and getting more work.

Good work ethic. Someone who is energetic, outgoing, enthusiastic, motivated, and gets the job at hand done will always be remembered!

Attractive. Let's face it; being attractive is a trait of the business. Even if you're not a supermodel, do your best to always be presentable. Shiny hair, a great smile, and amazing skin will go a long way.

Strong communication skills. You're going to have to talk to people, be friendly, and relay information to name a few assignments you may have. Being able to properly communicate is key.

Friendly. Companies and agencies are hiring you to be the "face" of the company. Companies need someone open, sincere and genuine.

Chapter 3: Q&A

What's in a name?

Being a promotional model can fall under an umbrella of several different categories, and your job can include a variety of things, so you will never be bored and always be learning new things! You may also be identified as:

*Model
*Convention model
*Promotional model
*Spokesmodel
*Hostess
*Brand ambassador
*In Store Demonstrator
*Tradeshow Demonstrator
*Crowd Gatherer
*Product specialist
*Product samplers
*Narrarator
*Costume character
*Event staff
*Street team

Where will I work?

*Tradeshows
*Conventions
*Car Shows
*Concerts
*County Fairs
*Festivals
*Grocery Stores
*Event launches
*Press Junkets
*In-store
* Award Shows
*Retail Stores/Shopping Malls
*Sporting Events
*Street Teams/Guerilla Marketing

What will I do?

*Create public interest in a product
*Crowd Gather
*Demonstrate
*Increase brand awareness
*Be the representative for the company
*Present information
*Gather information
*Hand out samples
*Hand out literature, brochures
*Hand out POS
*Promote the product
*Moderate contests
*Generate interest in the product
*Build current and future sales

Compensation

Compensation varies based on job, agent and client. The pay can vary from $15/hr-$30/hr for the average promo model or brand ambassador. Liquor and cigarette averages promos pay $20-$40/hr. Event managers and tour managers are paid usually a weekly flat rate from $700+. Product Specialists usually take home $700-$1500/day. Auto Show Specialists for automotive companies start at $300/day, with several contracted days per year. Tradeshow and Convention rates usually are between $200-$500/day.

What is a Promotional model?

The promo model is the consumer's first connection to the product or service. The promo model must know the product or service offered and is able to present the information to the consumer in a friendly, upbeat, and professional manner with the hope of gaining the customer's product loyalty.

Promotions are how many "real" models and actors actually make a living. Promotions range from being hired to hand out free samples of products to staffing trade shows booths in convention centers and tradeshows. This is a category that rarely involves being photographed and is very much about your personality and ability to interact with people.

Being a promo model means that you are brand ambassador for a certain company. Many companies hire temporary employees who they consider to be promotional models, for any given period of time. Contracts can be from one day to one year.

Promotional modeling covers a wide range of work for a promo girl including being on stands at exhibitions, handing out leaflets, or even being an 'Import Model'. (This is where you are booked at car, bike or import car race.) Good looks are important, however not the same kind of looks as for fashion models. The needs of clients that book promo models for this kind of work are completely different from a magazine client for example that wants a model that looks good in a beauty advertorial.

A promo model must be able to look good for long days without the help of makeup artists and retouching, be 'conventionally' good looking and represent their company with a friendly, successful image.

Whether the company is launching a new product, building a reputation or simply need a boost in sales...promotions is the key. Great marketing groups put together a creative plan and the promotional models carry it out.

A **Promotional Model** is a person hired to drive consumer demand for a product, service, brand, or concept by directly interacting with consumers. A promotional model can be female or male, and typically is attractive in physical appearance, and not only provides information to the consumer about the product or service, but makes it appealing to them in some way, enabling the consumer to identify with the product, service, or the company that offers it. While the length of interaction with the consumer may be short, the promotional model delivers a live experience that reflects on the product or service he or she is representing.

Even though this form of marketing touches fewer consumers per dollar spent than traditional advertising media (such as print, radio, and television) the consumer's perception of a brand, product, service, or company, is often more profoundly affected by a live person-to-person experience. The influence of this type of marketing campaign on consumer's purchasing habits tends to be more enduring as well. Promotional models often interact with many people per unit time so as to maximize quantitative influence on consumer demand. The responsibilities of the promotional model depend on the particular marketing campaign she or he is carrying out, and typically include but are not limited to the following:

1. Increasing product awareness
2. Creating an association in the consumer's mind between the product or brand and a particular idea (natural beauty, classic heritage, edgy sex appeal, reliability)
3. Providing product information
4. Handing items to consumers, such as a sample of the product itself, a small gift, or printed information

Marketing campaigns that make use of Promotional Models may take place in stores or malls, at tradeshows, special events, clubs, or even at outdoor public spaces. They are often planned at high traffic locations to reach as many consumers as possible, or at venues at which a particular type of target consumer is expected to be present.

Trade Show Models work a trade show floor space or booth, and represent a company to attendees. Trade Show Models are typically not regular employees of the company, but does the company renting the booth space hire freelancers. They are hired for several reasons. Trade Show Models make a company's booth more visibly distinguishable from the hundreds of other booths with which it competes for attendee attention. Also, Trade Show Models are articulate and quickly learn and explain or disseminate information on the company and its product and service, and can assist a company in handling a large number of attendees which the company might otherwise not have enough employees to accommodate, therefore increasing the number of sales or leads resulting from participation in the show. Trade Show Models can be skilled at drawing attendees into the booth, engaging them in conversation, and at spurring interest in the product, service, or company. Trade show models may be highly skilled at screening the mass of show attendees for target consumers or at obtaining attendee information so that they may be solicited after the show. Attire varies and depends on the nature of the show, and on the image the company would like to portray. They may wear a dress, or simple but flattering business attire. They sometimes wear wardrobe that is particular to the company, product, or service represented. The slang term 'Booth Babe' has occasionally been used to refer to a trade show model. The term focuses on physical appearance, or specifically on wardrobe, which, depending on the type of trade show can be thematic or sexy. For example, at a builder's convention a model may be dressed as a construction worker with cut-offs tight t-shirt, tool belt, and hardhat.

What is an independent contractor?

As an independent contractor, you are hired for certain events but are not employed by the company. Taxes are not taken out of your paycheck, and you are responsible for your own taxes at the end of the year. You will receive a 1099 at the end of the year and will file taxes accordingly. It is industry standard to fill out a W-9 for taxes with agency paperwork.

Chapter 4: Marketing

Basic Tools of the Trade

The necessities you will need to succeed in this business are:

*Positive attitude!
*Good work ethic.
*Good quality, professional pictures. (A good headshot and body shot for starters.)
*Cell phone.
*Email account.
*Business cards.
*Customer service experience.

Other options to maximize your marketing:
*Website.
*Fax machine.
*Headshots.
*Zed/comp cards.
*Sales experience.
*Laptop.
*Digital Camera.

To be the "Cream of the Crop"

*Always be on time!
*Always have a good attitude!
*Be professional at all times.
*Network!
*Wear EXACTLY what you have been instructed to wear.
*If you can help it, NEVER cancel!

Training

As a promo model, most training is done on site and with experience working in the field. For longer or more in depth accounts training is usually paid and done so the brand ambassador knows the product. In turn, this allows you to interact knowledgably with consumers. I do believe education is key in any field; so any other training you pursue on your own would help you. Public Speaking, Ear prompter and hosting are all class options to explore *if you choose*.

Clothing

The company will provide often clothing, but here is a list of things to keep on hand:

*Khaki pants
*Black dress pants
*Nice jeans
*White button down shirt
*Black tennis shoes
*CLEAN white tennis shoes

Ladies:
*Black heels
*Black boots
*Black fishnets

Chapter 5:
Word on the Street: Interviews

The Tour Manager

Name: Michelle Krishack

Job Position:
Experiential Mobile Marketing Asst. Tour Manager / DJ / Emcee

Job Description:
Writing detailed event recaps, keep watch on all staff during events, keep track of all tour inventory, handle all tour routing and hotel reservations, make sure tour stays inside all budgets, post finance (keeping receipts and formulate spreadsheets for tour company cards), keep clients happy, keep the husband I tour with happy and keep my arm within wine's reach at all times.

Best Part of Job: Travel
Worst Part of Job: Babysitting your crew

What do you look for in staff you hire?
Energy, enthusiasm, interest in the business if only for one day. We all understand you are not a professional promo model for life and we are absolutely certain at most times you would rather be somewhere else, but please entertain us and give us a smile, earn your money and bitch somewhere else.

Tips: The tips were said above, but overall. When I started out I realized that even though this business can be easy work, it still is work. It does not take much to do things correctly or even just do them the way your manager wants them to be done. Sometimes your manager has something in mind for the overall tour that a daily brand ambassador or promo model cannot see at this particular event they are working. Some managers even try new things out at their events, they may not work and the brand ambassador or promo model may (with a roll of their eyes) think this event is well..."lame".
Please entertain your managers, do the job, smile, get the paycheck and spend it on whatever you like ☺ the ones who this always get a call back.

The Promotional Model

Name: Kimberly Fisher

Job Position:
Promotional Model, Tradeshow Hostess and Product Specialist.

Job Description:
Being "the face" of certain products, from one day at a time to sometime several years. Interact with consumers, push brand awareness, and be friendly, outgoing and articulate.

Best Part of Job: Travel, meeting new people, never doing the same thing twice.
Worst Part of Job: Overbooking, sometimes-crazy schedule, deciding which jobs have priority.

What do you look for in a great promotional job?
A fun, organized company that loves what they do. Something that is interesting and rewarding. Reputable agencies that are not flaky, and pay on time!

Tips: A smile is worth a thousand words! Be friendly to everyone, you never know who could be the President or Senior VP of your company, or could be your next client. Even though you might work for a company for one day, you never know the referrals or future jobs it could bring, so always give it 110%! Network, network, network!

The Promotional Model

Name: Lina So

Job Position:

 Model/Actress

Job Description:

Casting, Booking, and producing for clients based on projects from tradeshows, events commercials, and ad campaigns.

Best Part of Job: Working with movers and shakers
Worst Part of Job: Time crunch and stressful

What do you look for in staff you hire:

We look for talent that is versatile, professional, punctual, and reliable. For live events it's extremely important to have friendly, outgoing, well-spoken models and narrators to engage buyers and clients into booth or draw attention to event. For print and commercial, experience is a must. Models need to know how to work camera, interact with other models, and take direction.

Tips: Work hard, play hard. Dot what you say you're going to do (have integrity) and be dependable and trust worthy all while looking good!

Chapter 6: The Good, the Bad & the Ugly

The Good

Doing trade shows and promotional jobs is a way to make a little cash on the side in between jobs for the avid model or aspiring actress. I've had my share of promotional and trade show experiences. I've worked in many types of industries that allowed me to explore the different audiences per industry and cities.

One company I have worked for many years was in the alarm industry. Picture a booth full of beautiful booth babes wearing business suits. The business attire required to wear were no ordinary business suits you see in a conservative catalog for business wear. Imagine short skirts, bare legs topped by high heels and lots of cleavage. Our job as spokesmodels was basically to smile and look pretty and attract people into the booth.

After the show was over, all spokesmodels had about 30-45 minutes to get dolled up in their hotel room and hit the town for the best five star restaurants in town. We also attended one or two networking functions before or after a plush dinner with gourmet food and the finest champagne and wines available to us. The limo bus picked us up from the hotel and we listened to high-energy music to set the tone for what would become a pretty fun night. Nothing tops the entertainment during some of this trade shows.

Carmen Garcia
Model and Writer

The Bad

I booked a job for a motorcycle company directly, and it was in San Francisco over the weekend. It sounded like a great gig; weekend in Napa Valley, luxury resort, great pay, easy workday and a great race.

When the other promo model and I arrived in San Francisco, we had to rent a car to drive to Napa. Needless to say, we were not very good with directs and the usual 2 hour drive took 4. When we finally arrived at the resort, we found out our room was the adjacent room to our boss' room. We had no idea that it would lead to him randomly knocking on our door at all hours! We actually spent most of the time pretending to be asleep or having the television up too loud to ignore him.

The job turned out ok, but it was a bit uncomfortable.

Lina So

The Ugly

   I took a job by a popular event company to host a Mercedes-Benz press junket for German auto writers visiting the United States. The position I applied for in LA was full, so I placed in Silver Lake, a small town halfway between Los Angeles and Las Vegas. I thought it would be a good chance to escape the city and have a mellow week.

   When I arrived at the dirty one star hotel, I realized it was about 30 miles from our actual destination, which was in the middle of nowhere. The gas expense they were covering didn't nearly cover half the cost of fuel they were providing. When we met our contact for the event, she was unorganized and asked rudely why we were late. We had showed up the exact time stated on our contract. (The hours she requested and the hours on our agency contract were different.) We later learned that we were not working our contracted hours but "would stay until released". At this point we called the agency because you must have approval for all overtime, if not they will not pay you. After 2 days of almost slave labor, the straw that broke the camels back was when I had to go back to LA for an audition. My booking agent asked me to go 30 miles out of the way, pick up the other model from the hotel and head to the job site. Adding 60 miles and 2 additional hours on to my trip seemed unreasonable, and I never was compensated for being a driver. I soon realized I was actually *losing* money working this job. We put in our notice that day and asked to be replaced. Our boss then asked up to drive 25 miles to the next city, drop off the wardrobe at the dry cleaners, pay for it and pick them back up and drop them off at the job site. Needless to say we did not.

   Not all jobs are what they are supposed to be! This was just one example of a "promo gone badly".

   Kimberly Fisher

Chapter 7:
Cyber Connections

The Agents

One great thing about being a promotional model is that you can sign up with each agent with a *non-exclusive* agreement. The more agents you have, the better your chance of getting work. The contacts below are from my years in the industry, referrals, and hours of independent research.

Key:
   * I have worked for the company.

   + I am listed with the company, but have not worked for them personally.

This list is invaluable! I have worked for several of these companies, so they are *legit* and *easy to work for.* I have also research other companies for you to sign up with.

Updated 01/11

Nationwide Promotional Agencies

- www.ActionEventPros.com+
- www.BDSMarketing.com*
- www.Belovedxp.com
- www.BigOrangeProductions.com+
- www.BishopProStaff.com (out of business)
- www.BrandStaffing.com (out of business)
- www.Campaigners.com
- www.CandyFord.com (out of business)
- www.CoasttoCoastModels.com
- www.CoolSideJobs.com
- www.DemosExpress.com
- www.DivaLeeProductions.com
- www.DrivenMarketingGroup.com (out of business)
- www.DrivenTalent.net
- www.DPTPromotions.com
- www.e-ventstaff.com
- www.EncoreNationwide.com
- www.Events-Promotions.com+
- www.EventProStrategies.com*
- www.EventNetUSA.com
- www.EventSpeak.com
- www.EventUS.com+
- www.EventUSMarketing.com+
- www.FemmePromotions.com
- www.frepm.com
- www.frontrow.ning.com
- www.theFusionTeam.com+
- www.GCMarketingServices.com*
- www.GMRMarketing.com
- www.GMRLive.com
- www.GreenHouseAgency.com
- www.GreetAmerica.com
- www.GT-Events.com
- www.HighClassPromotions.com (out of business)
- www.itmPromos.com
- www.Kandu-Marketing.com+
- www.Legacymp.com
- www.Level1Promotion.com
- www.Lpinstore.com
- www.MainEventsReporting.com+

- www.MakaiEvents.com
- www.MainEventsInc.com
- www.MarketStar.com
- www.MarketingWerks.com
- www.mcgconnect.com
- www.MobileMarketing.com
- www.MobileMarketing-Staffing.com
- www.MotherFunctionPR.com* (out of business)
- www.MG-Promotions.com (out of business)
- www.MMECasting.com
- www.MrYouth.com
- www.myPromoJobs.com+
- www.NationalEventStaffing.com+
- www.NationWideModels.com
- www.ncim.com+
- www.NextMarketing.com
- www.nrgSports.com (out of business)
- www.OntheMarkPromotions.com+
- www.OntheRocksModels.com
- www.RedLabelMarketing.com+ (out of business)
- www.RelayWorldwide.com
- www.rpmEventStaffing.com
- www.PFGEvents.com
- www.PictureU.com
- www.PoolModels.net+
- www.PromoGuys.com
- www.PromoModels.com
- www.Promo-Staff.com (out of business)
- www.PromoSynthesis.com+
- www.Promotion1.com
- www.PosStaffing.com
- www.PushModels.com
- www.RandolphStaffing.com (out of business)
- www.RedLightWorldwide.com
- www.RedPegRecruiting.com+
- www.RevolutionMarketing.com
- www.SnapShotPromotions.com+
- www.SohoExp.com
- www.SpokesmodelsPlus.com
- www.staffingexpressusa.com
- www.staffonmodels.com
- www.StayingConnected.com
- www.SteelAgency.com
- www.StratcoGroup.com

- www.StreetSampling.com (out of business)
- www.StreetTeamPromotion.com
- www.StreetTeamPromotion.jobs
- www.StuckforStaff.us+
- www.SupportbyRMD.com
- www.SweetDealin.com*
- www.TalentPoolInc.com
- www.thefemmeagency.com+
- www.thepetfirm.com
- www.thepinklight.com
- www.TheoAbbott.com+
- www.TSEstaffing.com
- www.TwoDotsProductions.com
- www.USConcepts.com+
- www.word13.com
- www.8DaysPromotions.com+
- www.5280Agency.com

Demonstration Staff
- www.gourmetdemo.com

Event Staff

- www.csc-usa.com

Regional Promotional Agencies:

- www.BostonBuzzz.com (New England)
- www.GoElite.com (Texas)
- www.MarketOneGroup.com (Texas)
- www.MidwestPromotionalStaffing.com (Chicago)
- www.ModelTalentOrlando.com (Florida)
- www.Nasco.ca (Canada)
- www.Nycastings.com (New York)
- www.PMGSuccess.com (Texas)
- www.KRULive.com (UK)

Nationwide Tradeshow Agencies:

- www.Anne-Obriant.com*
- www.AspenMarketing.com*
- www.CMTagency.com*
- www.ConventionConnection.com+
- www.etradeshowgirls.com
- www.ExpoStars.com+
- www.JwilliamsAgency.com*
- www.JudyVenn.com*
- www.KimLewis.com+ (retired)
- www.LBAssociates.com*
- www.MarlaDell.com
- www.MicheleandGroup.com
- www.ModelTalentOrlando.com
- www.Models4Tradeshows.com
- www.PatrickTalent.com*
- www.Productions-Plus.com*
- www.SpokesmodelsPlus.com*
- www.StatementModels.com
- www.Tradeshow-Visions.com+ (out of business)
- www.1stPlaceModels.com

Local Vegas Agencies:

- www.Baskow.com*
- www.BestModelsandTalent.com*
- www.CoolBlueTalent.com
- www.CreativeImageAgency.com
- www.EnvyModelTalent.com*
- www.FarringtonProductions.com
- www.Gacasting.com+
- www.HarperTalent.com+
- www.HolidayModels.com+
- www.IconLV.com*
- www.Impact-Models.com* (out of business)
- www.LangeAgency.com
- www.LenzTalent.com
- www.LVTalent.com+
- www.LVTalentAgency.com+
- www.MetroModels.info
- www.PromosnVegas.com
- www.RedAgencylv.com*
- www.SinCityCaddyGirls.com+
- www.TruTalentManagement.com
- www.VictoriasEventProduction.com+ (out of business)
- www.VegasHotties.com+
- www.VegasHotBodies.com

Chapter 8: Resources

Photographers:
www.beautybydivini.com
www.brunotalledo.com
www.tdphoto.com
www.toddtyler.com

Free Model Pages/Websites:
www.modelmayhem.com
www.imodel.com
www.onemodelplace.com

Tax Info:
W9 Form (www.**irs.gov**/pub/irs-pdf/fw9.pdf)

Sample Contract #1

TALENT CONTRACT

TODAY'S DATE:	Jan 5, 2010
MODEL/TALENT:	
COMPANY/CLIENT:	Engage Partners
CONTACT (S):	Art
SHOW/EVENT:	CES company party
JOB FUNCTION:	Mix/Mingle Hostess
LOCATION:	Blush at Wynn
MEET AT:	Meet Art (or Leana 743-4964 from Impact) outside of Daniel Boulud Restaurant in the Wynn at 9:45pm

YOUR AGENT: Carla DiBlasi / PHONE #'s: Agency – 702-319-3001 cell# 702-296-1388/ FX 702-319-3002

PLEASE CALL ASAP IF YOU HAVE ANY PROBLEMS REGARDING THIS BOOKING

Job Date	Day	Arrival Time	Start Time	End Time	Total Hrs.	Rate	Total Rate
Jan 6'10	Wed	9:45p	10pm	2am	4 hrs	$36/hr	$144

TOTAL TO YOU / TALENT: $144.00

**WARDROBE: nightclub attire

TALENT NAME	
ADDRESS	
PHONE NUMBER	
SOC. SEC. NUMBER	

I, _____ _ agree to work for the above-mentioned client under the terms and conditions stated in the "INDEPENDENT CONTRACTOR" agreement which I signed with IMPACT MODELS AND ENTERTAINMENT. I also understand that if I do not show up for this job or if I show up late with / without proper notification, I am held responsible for Impact Model's lost agency fees due to my absence and / or tardiness. . If the Client should cancel talent and/or the job booking, this contract is null and void.

This confirmation / contract serves as an agreement that the above talent signing agrees to work for this client exclusively through IMPACT MODELS & ENTERTAINMENT for the next three (3) years. This means that I, as talent, cannot work directly for this client or through another agency for 3 years. This includes all trade shows, promotions, print or commercial assignments. Legal action can and will be taken against me if I do. I also understand that I will be paid from IMPACT MODELS & ENTERTAINMENT once they have received payment from the Company/ client.

Carla DiBlasi 01/05/10

| TALENT SIGNATURE | DATE | IMPACT MODELS & ENTERTAINMENT DATE |

The Labor Commission of Nevada licenses this agency.

Tel 702.319.3001 fax 702.319.3002   3450 E Russell rd. #104 LV NV 89120 impact-models.com

43

Chapter 9: Special Thanks

Special Thanks:

www.LinaSo.com
For being a great friend, confidante, book contributor, booker, partner in crime and "little sister"! You have always been there for me, from Vegas to LA to Brazil to Bahamas and back! You are the best!

www.DiviniRae.com
We have had such amazing times and we have grown, evolved, and remained friends since those memorable days in Cabo. Thank you for your artistic creativity, inner and outer beauty and open-minded friendship.

www.Shantelle.net
From Asian bikini team to teaching English in Spain to New Years in Jamaica…our adventures are endless! You inspired me to write this book and I couldn't have had a better "Super Role Model!" Here's to our next journey!

Jonathan Miller for all of the writing tips, advice, edits and many Los Angeles lunches. Your work as a writer has inspired me!

To all of my friends and family, I could not have picked a better bunch.

To all of my booking agents and promotional agents that gave me the chance (and material!) to work in such a great industry.

To my chapter cover models for use of our images; 1.) Shari, Lana 2.) Line 3.) Chi 4.) Rocky, Madison, Z, Lina 5.) The Girls of CES 08/Sony 6.) Shana, Misti 7.) Rebecca 8.) Sarah 9.) Lina

Notes:

Notes:

To purchase additional copies of this book directly, go to
www.KimberlyFisher.com and click on "Promotional Modeling 101".